Copyright   Bakthi Ross © 2017

Waxwing publishing

All rights reserved

No part of this book may be reproduced or transmitted in any form or by any means, electronic or mechanical, including photocopying, recording, or by any information storage and retrieval system without permission in writing from the author.

Author Bakthi Ross © 2017.08.17

For information or to order additional books, please write to

Waxwing

PO Box 373

MORAYFIELD 4506

AUSTRALIA

OR PHONE 07-54987214

ISBN 978 1 922220 35 6

My Dad Was a Puff

By Bakthi Ross

 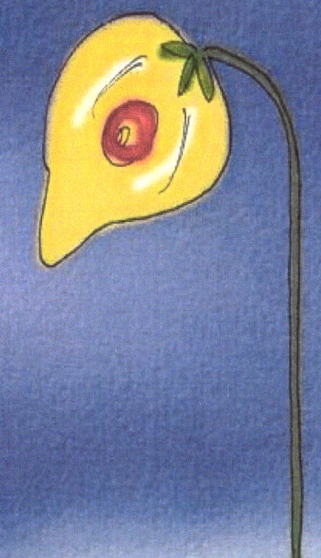

My dad was a puff and
he hid behind the smoke.

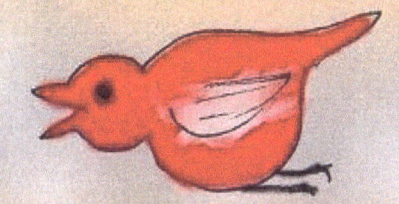

He blew smoke and the smoke flew all around.

Some days the smoke rolled like a wind.

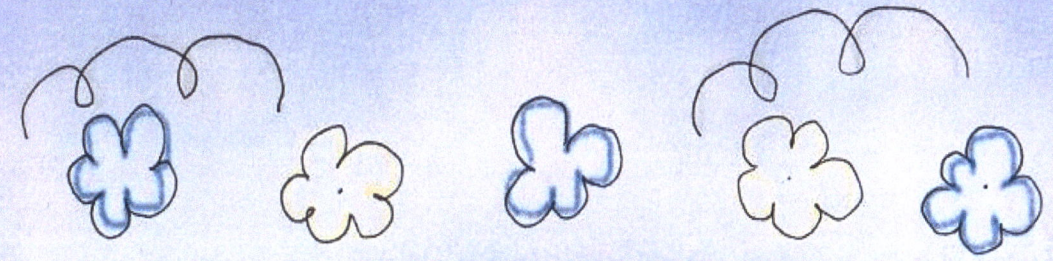

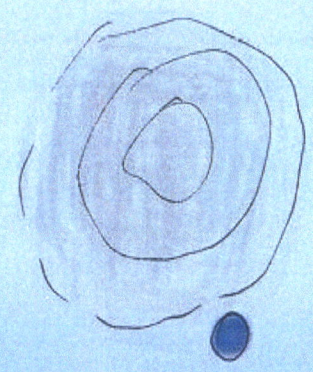
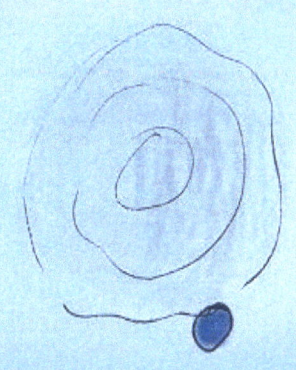

Some days the smoke
blew in streaks.

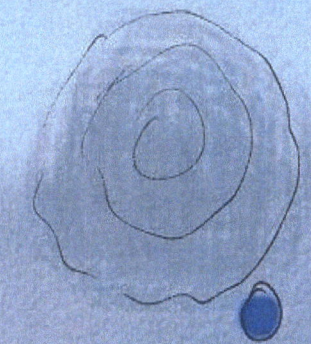
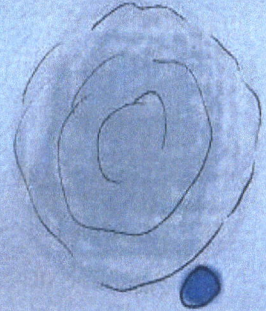

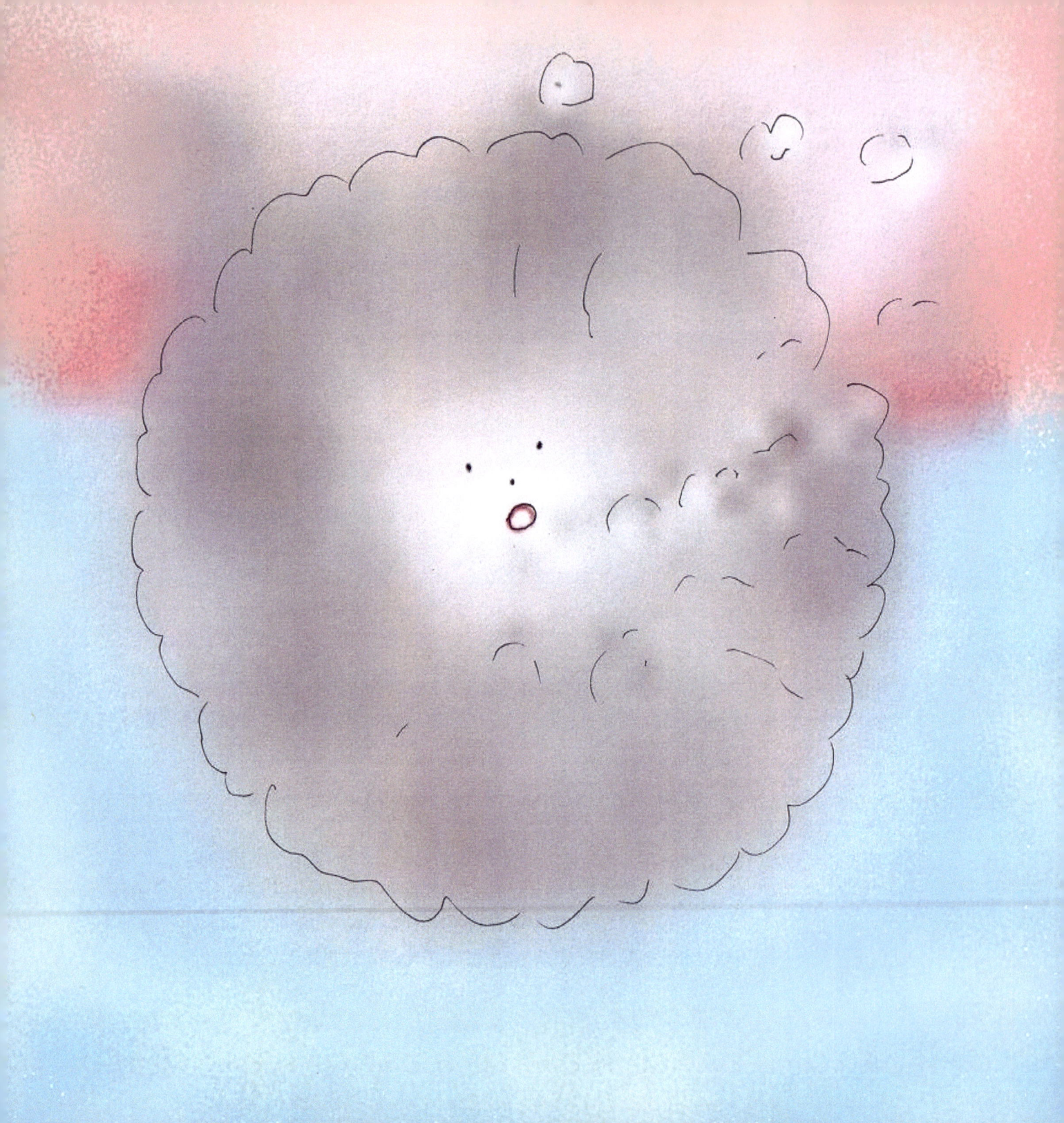

He sat inside a black cloud.

I wanted to hold his hands but he had only one hand free.

I didn't like my dad living inside the dark clouds.

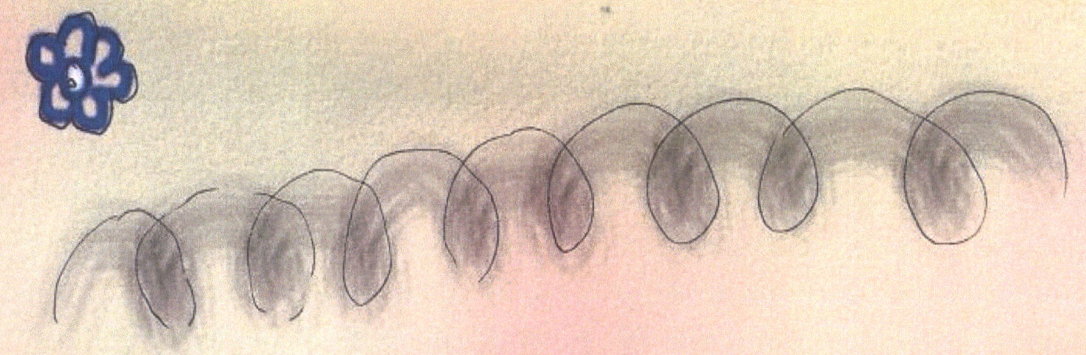

So I pulled him. He refused. Then I pulled him again.

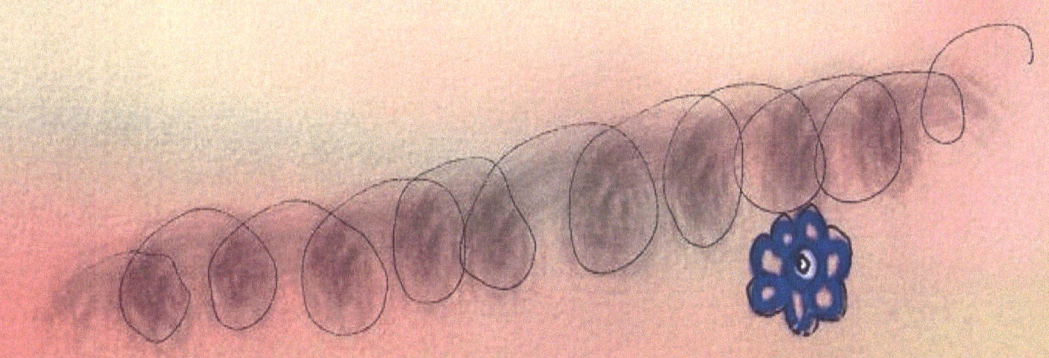

I took him to the park.

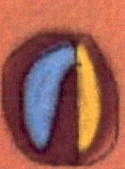

We played together and watched the birds.

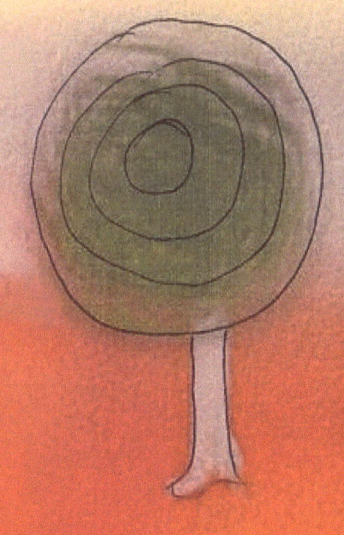
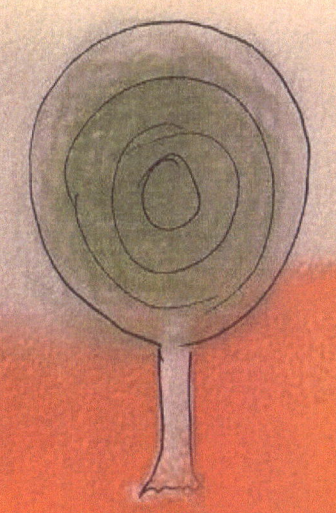

His both hands were free.

He came out of the black smoke and enjoyed the outdoors. He was free from his dark clouds.

www.ingramcontent.com/pod-product-compliance
Lightning Source LLC
Chambersburg PA
CBHW041541040426
42446CB00002B/183